This book belongs to:

First Edition

ISBN-10: 1-68063-052-0
ISBN-13: 978-1-68063-052-7

Published by
Myrddin Publishing Group
Contact us at - www.myrddinpublishing.com

Myrddin Publishing

Disclaimer
Although the author and publisher have made every effort to ensure that the information in this book was correct at press time, the author and publisher do not assume and hereby disclaim any liability to any party for any loss, damage, or disruption caused by errors or omissions, whether such errors or omissions result from negligence, accident, or any other cause.

Under the Sea Puzzles

Minkie Monster and the Lost Treasure

Ceri Clark

Visit **MinkieMonster.com** to get another children's book for free!

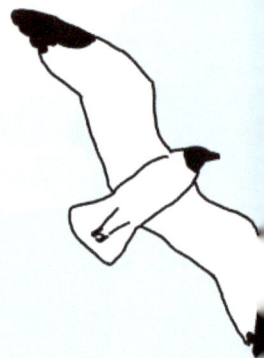

Dedication
I would like to dedicate this book to Alison, Connie, Jenny and NIck, without whom I could not have made it.

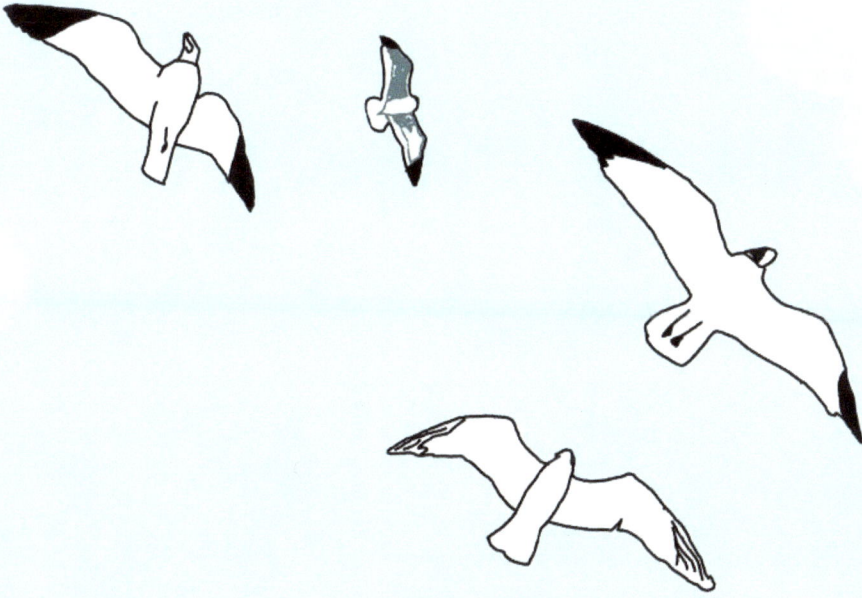

Note for Parents

This book is designed to engage children from the ages of 3 to 5. The puzzles at the beginning are aimed at the lower age group but they get progressively harder to keep them interested as they get older.

There is a link in the middle of this book that will take you to the author's website where you can download a PDF version so that you can print out these puzzles to be used again and again.

This book has puzzles to stimulate your child's creativity and cognitive ability as well as practice their reading and counting.

The best way to use this book, is to give them a set of pens and let them loose on the pages while giving them hints and some advice if they get stuck.

There is **treasure** in the sea,
I will **find** it, you will see.
Gold and silver, coins and cups,
there is **no** need for grownups.

How many
birds can you see?

Oh **WOW**, the sea is so beautiful,
I am missing **Bob** as usual.
He is waiting by the ship for **me**.
We only have one **key**, you see.

See you later Bob!

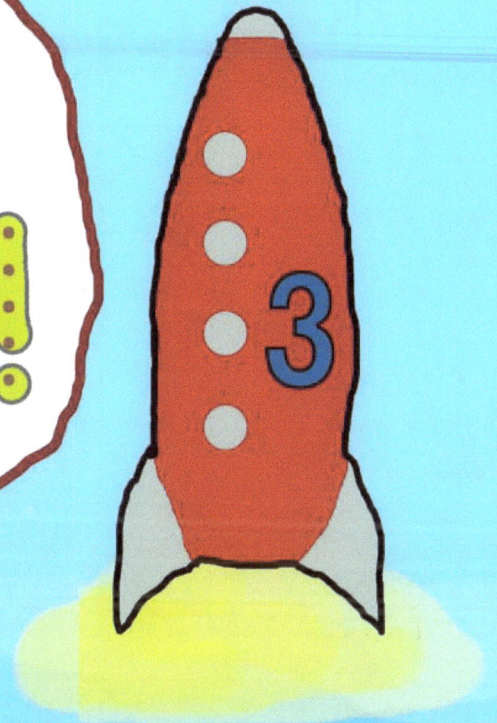

Trace the letters to say goodbye to Bob.

Oh no, I have lost control.
The tide is strong, I'm in tow.
I am lost, I don't know where I am.
I need help to get out of this jam.

1 2 3 4 5 6 7 8 9 10

Minkie is scared, help him to count to ten to calm him down by tracing the numbers.

"Hello, my dear, are you **lost?**" the turtle asked.
"I am. The tide took me far, this sea is **vast**."
"Sorry, I **cannot** go with you but go straight on."
"A sea horse can help you by the name of **John**."

Spot the 3 differences in the ships.

"John, can you help? Do you know where the treasure is?"
"I do not but I know who might, a fish called Liz.
She is an angel fish.
She can help you with your wish."

Time to get your crayons out!

"I see treasure is **not** what you are really looking for. Look **beyond** the reef, the canyon, on the great sea floor."

With her nose, she drew a **map** in the sand,
"**Go now**, I see a shark is also coming,"
came the demand.

Treasure

Can you find your way to the treasure?

Towards the reef I swam.
A Shark! Oh no, I must scram!
There is a shadow below,
I am suddenly scared.
I must swim to the surface or I will not be
spared.

W	H	A	L	E			
S	E	A	H	O	R	S	E
O	C	T	O	P	U	S	K
F	I	S	H				R
							A
N	I	H	P	L	O	D	H
T	U	R	T	L	E		S
H	S	I	F	R	A	T	S

Turtle
Dolphin
Fish
Octopus
Whale
Shark
Starfish
Seahorse

Find the sea creatures in the word search!

Oh where is Bob? I miss him,
I think as I quickly swim.

I break out of the water to the **sound** of a screech.
It takes me a second to realize it is **speech**.

Join the dots
to draw
the ship.

"What are you? I've not seen **anything** like you before."

He looked around from left to right, "Are there **any more?**"

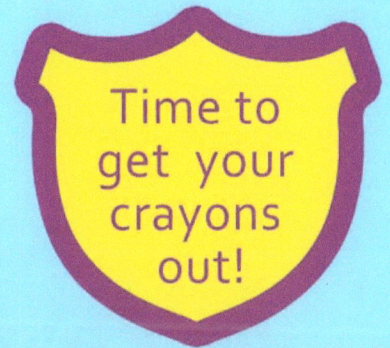

Time to get your crayons out!

It tilted its head, its eyes were **big** and **wide.**

"I am Minkie Monster, will you be my **guide?**"

He answered with a **screech,**
and he **flew** out of reach.
I **turned** slowly — there was something **behind me.**
A **giant** octopus rose out of the sea.

How many legs
does the Octopus have?

I swam for **hours** in the sparkling water.

All the time, getting more tired and **hotter**.

Yay, I see a **swordfish** in the distance.

Maybe he could give me some **assistance?**

A yellow fish and starfish swam away from the pattern. Which fish goes where?

I can't **catch** him, he is out of sight.
I call out loud,
"Come back! I won't **bite!**"

Minkie met a lot of friends on his journey. Can you match the creatures to their shadows?

There is a large shadow below.
I am scared, it is a shark I know.

The shark's teeth are so **big and white.**
His jaws open **wide,**
he will bite!

Is that **Bob** over there?
Yes! Take that! Sharks beware!

Trace the letters to help Bob.

BASH

The scary shark fled.
"You are safe," Bob said.

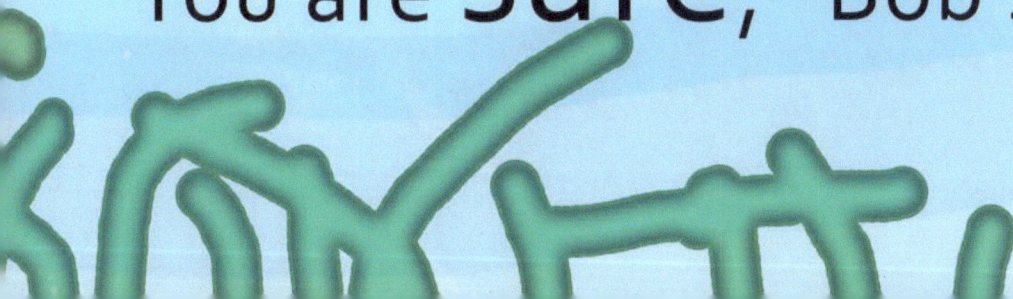

I have found my **real** treasure —
my best friend
Bob.

Hugging friends
both new and
old is far better
than treasure of
silver and gold!

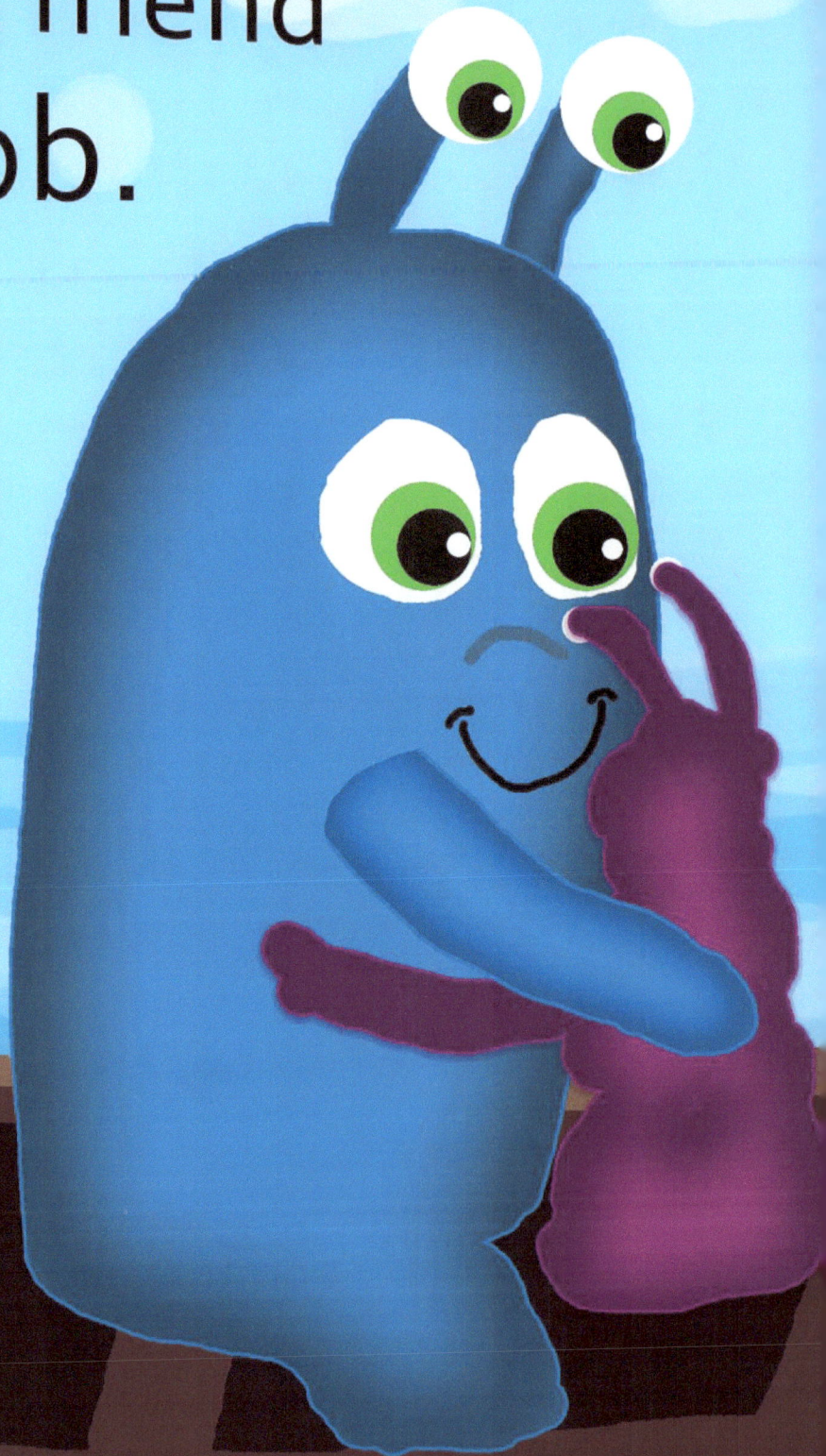

F	R	I	E	N	D
	H	E	L	P	N
			V		U
E	F	A	S		O	F
S	E	M	A	G	L

Friend   Love   Fun
Games   Help   Safe

Find the words in the Puzzle!

About Ceri Clark

Ceri Clark lives in the Land of Myth with her husband and young son. She spent time as a school librarian but now loves to create puzzles and stories for children of all ages.

Visit **MinkieMonster.com** to get another children's book for free!

Please consider leaving a review,
A few words or more that are true.
I appreciate it takes time,
but it would be really sublime.
For now adieu and most of all, thank you.

SPACE PUZZLES
MINKIE MONSTER AND THE BIRTHDAY SURPRISE
Ceri Cl...

UNDER THE SEA PUZZLES
MINKIE MONSTER AND THE LOST TREASURE
Ceri Clark

SPACE
A MINKIE MONSTER COLORING BOOK
Ceri Clark

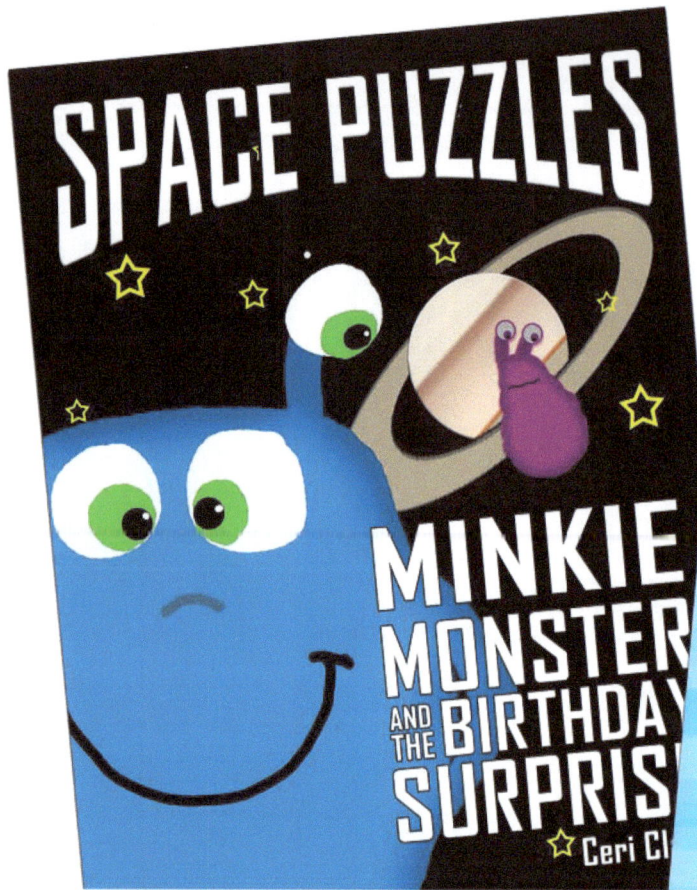

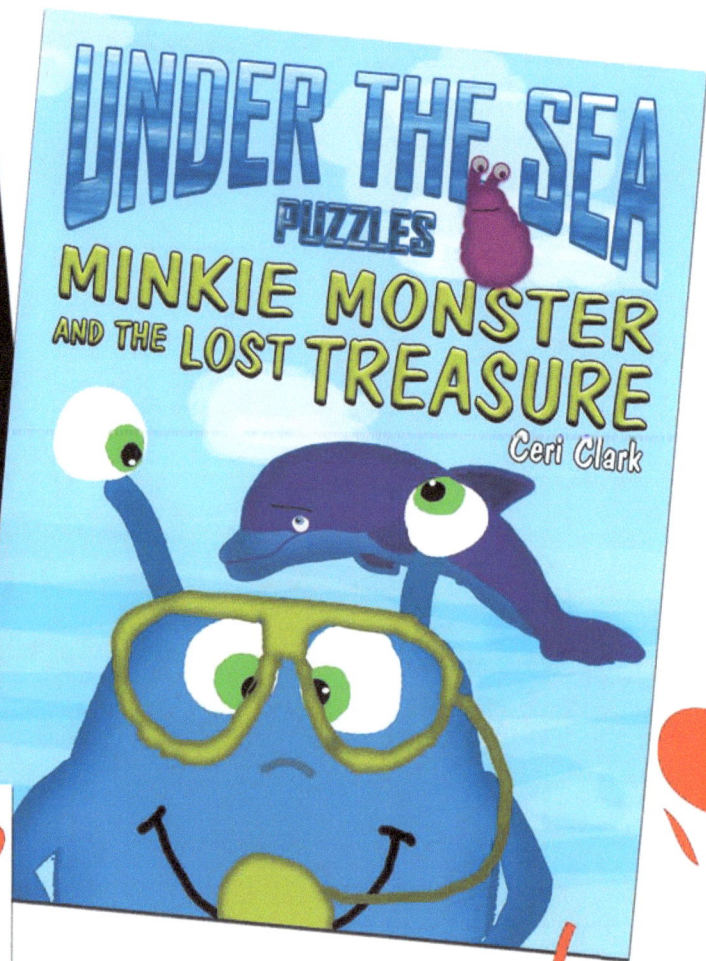

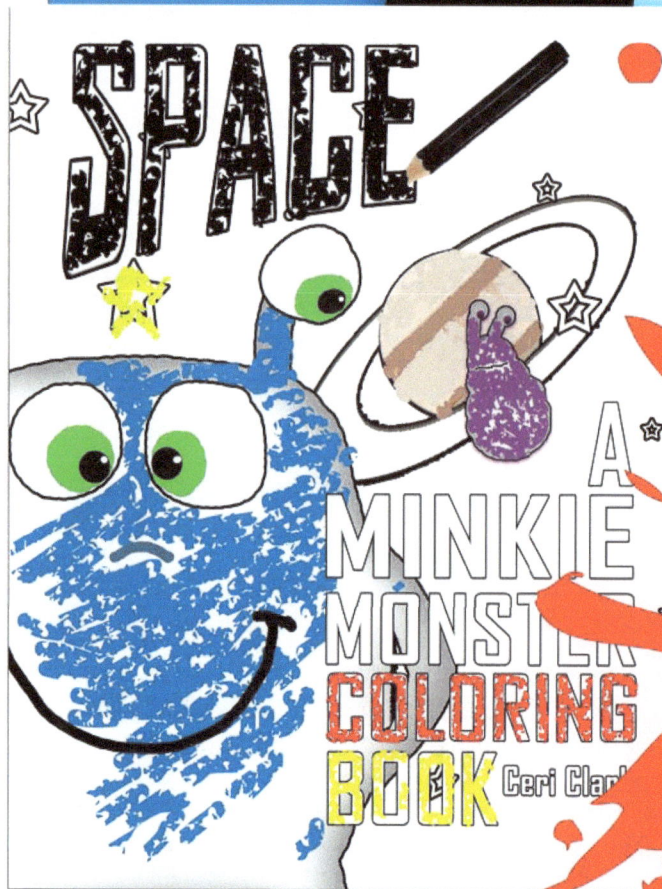

www.ingramcontent.com/pod-product-compliance
Lightning Source LLC
LaVergne TN
LVHW072121070426
835511LV00002B/52